**Illustrated by
Dan Green**

Designed and produced by
Autumn Publishing Ltd
Chichester, West Sussex, UK PO20 7EQ

© 2005 Autumn Publishing Ltd

Printed in Spain

ISBN 1 84531 144 2

**BYEWAY
B O O K S**

KICK OFF! 2 times table

You can have as much fun with the times tables as you can with football league tables! Let's kick off with the 2 times table. Diego Primadonna, striker for Aston Vanilla, has to count the pairs of boots by counting in **2s**. Can you help him? Colour every 2nd boot as you count.

$1 \times 2 = \boxed{2}$

$2 \times 2 = \square$

Counting in twos can help you with your 2 times table. Look at the boots you have coloured in to help you complete the 2 times table. Then, finish drawing the pairs of knobbly knees!

$3 \times 2 = \square$

$4 \times 2 = \square$

$5 \times 2 = \square$

NOTICE HOW ALL OF YOUR ANSWERS ARE EVEN NUMBERS! NOW TRY LEARNING THE 2 TIMES TABLE. COVER IT WITH A PIECE OF PAPER AND SEE HOW MANY YOU CAN REMEMBER. NO PEEKING!

$6 \times 2 = \square$

$7 \times 2 = \square$

$8 \times 2 = \square$

$9 \times 2 = \square$

$10 \times 2 = \square$

Now check your answers at the back of the book and write your number of goals scored (correct answers) on the ball.

Can you work out the answers to these sock sums by using the 2 times table?

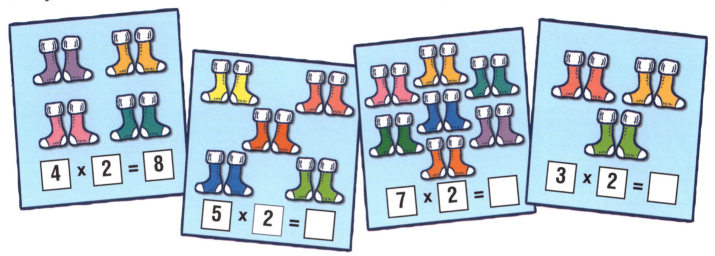

$4 \times 2 = 8$

$5 \times 2 = \square$

$7 \times 2 = \square$

$3 \times 2 = \square$

Fill in the missing numbers on the shirts.

$\square \times 2 = 10$

$\square \times 2 = 20$

$7 \times \square = 14$

$9 \times \square = 18$

$\square \times 2 = 8$

$\square \times 2 = 12$

Back of the net

Use your 2 times tables to join the dots and complete this goal-scoring moment.

2

16

4

14

6

12

20   18

10   8

Check your answers and write your goal score here!

3 times table

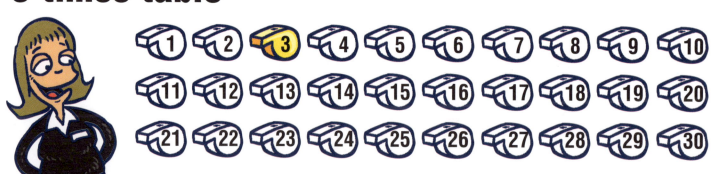

This referee keeps her whistle from every game as a souvenir. Colour every 3rd whistle as you count.

Action Replay

Look at the whistles you have coloured in to help you complete the 3 times table below. Then, finish adding the missing balls into the bags!

NOW TRY LEARNING THE 3 TIMES TABLE. COVER IT WITH A PIECE OF PAPER AND SEE HOW MANY YOU CAN REMEMBER.

1 x 3 = 3

2 x 3 =

3 x 3 =

4 x 3 =

5 x 3 =

6 x 3 =

7 x 3 =

8 x 3 =

9 x 3 =

10 x 3 =

Add up your goals!

World Cup winners

Using what you already know about the 3 times tables, work out the total number of stripes on these World Cup winners' flags.

3 x 3 = 9

☐ x ☐ = ☐

☐ x ☐ = ☐

☐ x ☐ = ☐

Fill in the missing numbers on these corner flags.

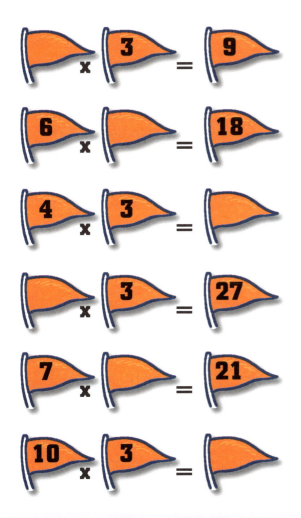

☐ x 3 = 9

6 x ☐ = 18

4 x 3 = ☐

☐ x 3 = 27

7 x ☐ = 21

10 x 3 = ☐

Corner kick

Here's your chance to take a corner and score an extra goal! Colour in all the shapes with numbers in the 3 times table and see if you can make it to the top of the league!

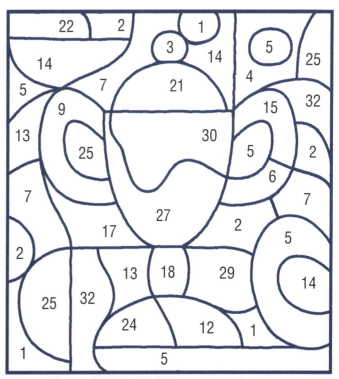

How many did you score?

4 times table

If you know your 2 times table, then it's easy to learn your 4s – all you have to do is double the 2s!
So, if **2 x 2 = 4** then **2 x 4 = 8,** and if **5 x 2 = 10** then **5 x 4 = 20.**

Garth Time of Aston Vanilla loves eating! He's particularly fond of the half-time oranges and can eat at least four pieces every game. Colour every 4th orange as you count.

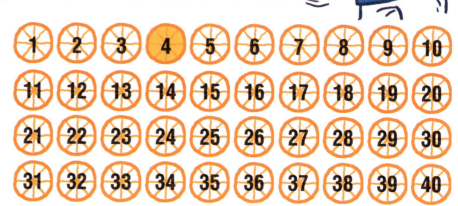

1 | 2 | 3 | 4 | 5 | 6 | 7 | 8 | 9 | 10
11 | 12 | 13 | 14 | 15 | 16 | 17 | 18 | 19 | 20
21 | 22 | 23 | 24 | 25 | 26 | 27 | 28 | 29 | 30
31 | 32 | 33 | 34 | 35 | 36 | 37 | 38 | 39 | 40

Action Replay

Now try filling in the answers to the 4 times table. Then, add the missing stripes to the shirts.

NOTICE HOW ALL THE NUMBERS ARE EVEN NUMBERS – JUST LIKE THE 2 TIMES TABLE. NOW TRY LEARNING THE 4 TIMES TABLE. COVER IT WITH A PIECE OF PAPER AND SEE HOW MANY YOU CAN REMEMBER.

1 x 4 = 4

2 x 4 =

3 x 4 =

4 x 4 =

5 x 4 =

6 x 4 =

7 x 4 =

8 x 4 =

9 x 4 =

10 x 4 =

How did you do?

Use the 4 times table to write the multiplication sums for these pictures.

2 x 4 = 8

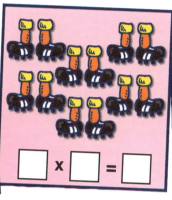

☐ x ☐ = ☐

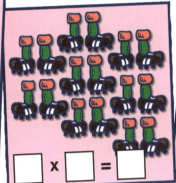

☐ x ☐ = ☐

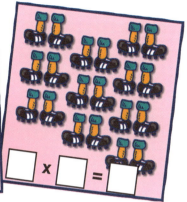

☐ x ☐ = ☐

Fill in the missing numbers on these red and yellow cards.

☐ x 4 = 8

☐ x 4 = 24

4 x ☐ = 16

4 x ☐ = 40

3 x 4 = ☐

4 x 5 = ☐

On the ball

Solve the multiplication sums and follow the code to colour the ball.

4 - red
8 - green
12 - blue
16 - pink
20 - black

24 - orange
28 - white
32 - brown
36 - purple
40 - grey

7 x 4
4 x 4
3 x 4
5 x 4
10 x 4
8 x 4
1 x 4
2 x 4
9 x 4
6 x 4

How many did you score?

5 times table

Your 5 times table is as easy as a free kick with Benito 'Butterfingers' Bolero in goal! All of the answers end in either **0** or **5**.

1	2	3	4	5	6	7	8	9	10
11	12	13	14	15	16	17	18	19	20
21	22	23	24	25	26	27	28	29	30
31	32	33	34	35	36	37	38	39	40
41	42	43	44	45	46	47	48	49	50

Colour every 5th box in the goal net as you count.

Now work out the answers to the 5 times table. Then, add the missing fingers to the goalie gloves.

HOW DID YOU DO? DID YOU NOTICE THE PATTERN? TRY LEARNING THE TABLE BY HEART NOW.

1 x 5 = 5

2 x 5 = ☐

3 x 5 = ☐

4 x 5 = ☐

5 x 5 = ☐

6 x 5 = ☐

7 x 5 = ☐

8 x 5 = ☐

9 x 5 = ☐

10 x 5 = ☐

Are you a super striker yet? Add up your shots at goal.

If a star equals 5 points, how many points has each team earned?

Aston Vanilla	★ ★ ★	3 x 5 = 15
Inter Myflan	★ ★ ★ ★ ★	☐ x ☐ = ☐
Ramshackle Rovers	★ ★	☐ x ☐ = ☐
Pretend Madrid	★ ★ ★ ★ ★ ★ ★ ★ ★	☐ x ☐ = ☐

Which team has the **most** points? ☐

Which team has the **least** points? ☐

• •

Extra time

How did these wingers do? Write the answers to the multiplication sums in the correct goals.

3 x 5

6 x 5

5 x 7

8 x 5

Did you play a blinder? Add your score.

6 times table

The 6 times table may seem tricky, but remember, multiplication sums have the same answer whichever way round you write them.

So, **6 x 2 = 12** and **2 x 6 = 12**. Because you have already learned your 2, 3, 4 and 5 times tables, you already know half of your 6 times table. Game on!

Colour every 6th flag as you count the numbers.

Now work out the answers to the 6 times table. Use the table above to help you if you need it. Add the missing spots to the footballs when you have finished.

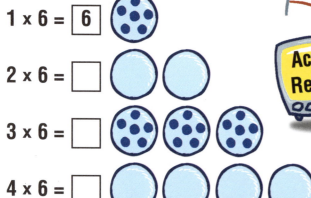

1 x 6 = 6

2 x 6 =

3 x 6 =

4 x 6 =

5 x 6 =

6 x 6 =

7 x 6 =

8 x 6 =

9 x 6 =

10 x 6 =

HOW DID YOU DO? DID YOU NOTICE THE PATTERN? TRY LEARNING THE TABLE OFF BY HEART NOW.

Are you a super striker yet? Add up your shots at goal.

Team tactics

Ivor Ticlykovv, manager of Inter Myflan, has been discussing team tactics for the next game.
He wants to keep them secret. Use the code to work out the tactics.

E	D	O	F	T	R	A	S	P	I
60	48	12	30	24	18	36	6	0	54

1. **2 x 6**
2. **5 x 6**
3. **5 x 6**
4. **1 x 6**
5. **9 x 6**
6. **8 x 6**
7. **10 x 6**
8. **4 x 6**
9. **3 x 6**
10. **6 x 6**
11. **0 x 6**

1. O	2.	3.	-	4.	5.	6.	7.

8.	9.	10.	11.

HALF-TIME WHISTLE

You're half-way to becoming top of the times tables! The whistle has blown and it's time to take a much-deserved break.

Prawnio, Inter Myflan's team mascot, has run onto the pitch with three buckets of half-time oranges. He has sliced each orange in half, then cut each half into 6 pieces. Work out how many pieces there are in each bucket. The first bucket has been done for you.

2 oranges

$2 \times 2 = 4$ halves

$4 \times 6 = 24$ pieces

4 oranges

☐ x ☐ = ☐ halves

☐ x ☐ = ☐ pieces

5 oranges

☐ x ☐ = ☐ halves

☐ x ☐ = ☐ pieces

What's your half-time score?

HALF-TIME ANALYSIS

Let's see how you're getting on and do a quick action replay of the tables you have learned so far.

In a spin

Aston Vanilla's number one fan, Brad Lucke, has offered to wash the team shirts, but has got into a bit of a spin. The shirts are going in with one number on them, and coming out with another! Write the new numbers on the shirts.

Trophy takers

Join the dots to see which trophy each team bagged.

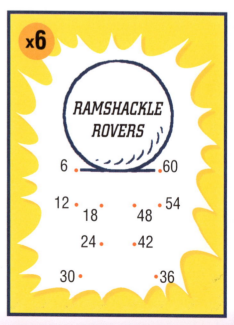

How did you do?

Get dribbling!

Follow the paths of these dribblers, by matching the numbered cones to each player.

SO HOW HAVE YOU SCORED IN THE FIRST HALF OF THE GAME? DON'T WORRY IF YOU'RE NOT ON TOP FORM YET – REMEMBER, FOOTBALL IS A GAME OF TWO HALVES! NOW BACK TO THE GAME.

7 times table

Colour in every 7th sponge as you count the numbers in the grid.

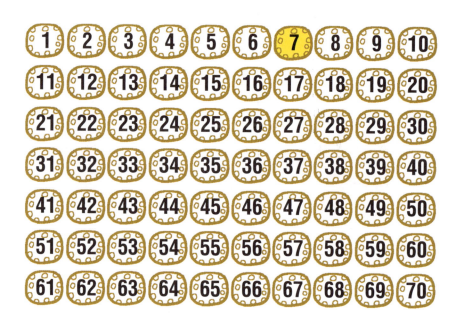

1	2	3	4	5	6	7	8	9	10
11	12	13	14	15	16	17	18	19	20
21	22	23	24	25	26	27	28	29	30
31	32	33	34	35	36	37	38	39	40
41	42	43	44	45	46	47	48	49	50
51	52	53	54	55	56	57	58	59	60
61	62	63	64	65	66	67	68	69	70

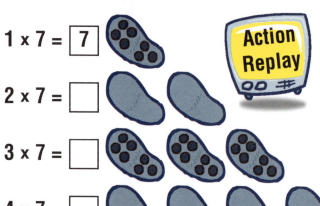

Action Replay

Use the grid to help you with your 7 times table. Remember, you already know the answers to the first 6 sums in the table… just swap the numbers in the sums around and you'll be player of the match! Add the missing studs to the boots.

WAS THE NUMBER 7 LUCKY FOR YOU? COVER THE TABLE UP AND SEE IF YOU CAN REMEMBER IT WITHOUT LOOKING.

1 x 7 = 7

2 x 7 =

3 x 7 =

4 x 7 =

5 x 7 =

6 x 7 =

7 x 7 =

8 x 7 =

9 x 7 =

10 x 7 =

Add up your shots at goal.

Sliding tackles

☐ x ☐ = ☐

☐ x ☐ = ☐

☐ x ☐ = ☐

☐ x ☐ = ☐

Bowen Crusher, wearing number 7 for Pretend Madrid, has been playing dirty again! In his last game against Aston Vanilla, Bowen committed four sliding tackles! Here they are freeze-framed. Multiply the numbers on the players' shirts.

Keepy-uppy

Misty Target has been practising her ball control – except she doesn't seem to have much of it! Circle the balls that are in the 7 times table.

63 14 45

42 49 5

61 16

35 11 7 21

55 56

70 27

How did you do?

8 times table

ALL OF THE NUMBERS IN THE 8 TIMES TABLE ARE EVEN. COLOUR EVERY 8TH BOX AS YOU COUNT.

1	2	3	4	5	6	7	8	9	10
11	12	13	14	15	16	17	18	19	20
21	22	23	24	25	26	27	28	29	30
31	32	33	34	35	36	37	38	39	40
41	42	43	44	45	46	47	48	49	50
51	52	53	54	55	56	57	58	59	60
61	62	63	64	65	66	67	68	69	70
71	72	73	74	75	76	77	78	79	80

Action Replay

See how you get on tackling the 8 times table. If you get stuck, finish cutting the orange halves into 8 pieces to help you work out the answers. Cover up the table and try learning it.

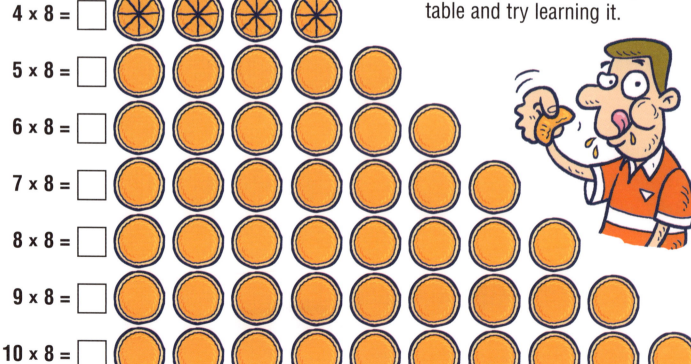

1 x 8 = 8

2 x 8 =

3 x 8 =

4 x 8 =

5 x 8 =

6 x 8 =

7 x 8 =

8 x 8 =

9 x 8 =

10 x 8 =

Add up your score for the page.

Fever pitch!

Temperatures have risen at the Old Triffid stadium, as the Aston Vanilla team have lost their kits! Match the players to the kits to save their blushes!

PENALTY KICK

Here's your chance to have a few extra shots at goal and earn some more points. Fill in the numbers to complete the multiplication sums in the goal.

x	3	4	5	6		x	5	6	7	8
2						8				
3		12				7				
4						6		36		
5						5				

Did you score? Add up your points.

9 times table

COLOUR IN EVERY 9TH ROSETTE AS YOU COUNT THE NUMBERS.

1	2	3	4	5	6	7	8	9	10
11	12	13	14	15	16	17	18	19	20
21	22	23	24	25	26	27	28	29	30
31	32	33	34	35	36	37	38	39	40
41	42	43	44	45	46	47	48	49	50
51	52	53	54	55	56	57	58	59	60
61	62	63	64	65	66	67	68	69	70
71	72	73	74	75	76	77	78	79	80
81	82	83	84	85	86	87	88	89	90

Action Replay

1 x 9 = 9

2 x 9 =

3 x 9 =

4 x 9 =

5 x 9 =

6 x 9 =

7 x 9 =

8 x 9 =

9 x 9 =

10 x 9 =

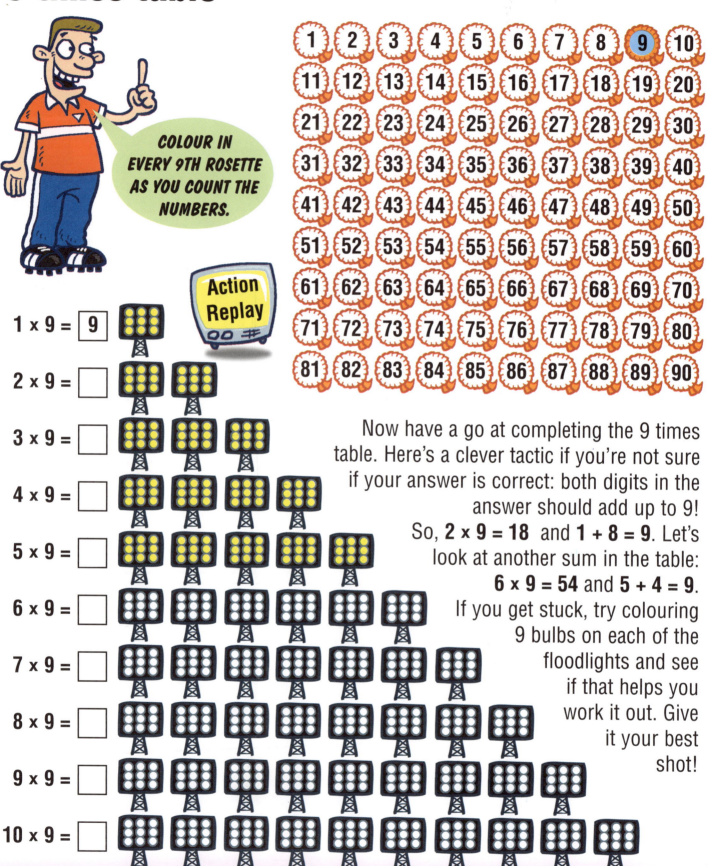

Now have a go at completing the 9 times table. Here's a clever tactic if you're not sure if your answer is correct: both digits in the answer should add up to 9! So, **2 x 9 = 18** and **1 + 8 = 9**. Let's look at another sum in the table: **6 x 9 = 54** and **5 + 4 = 9**. If you get stuck, try colouring 9 bulbs on each of the floodlights and see if that helps you work it out. Give it your best shot!

Cover up the table and try learning it off by heart.

How did you do?

Spot the balls

Spot the balls in the grid and work out the answers to the multiplications by going across the grid then down. With times tables, you can swap the numbers in the sums around, so you could go up the grid then across it to find the sum!

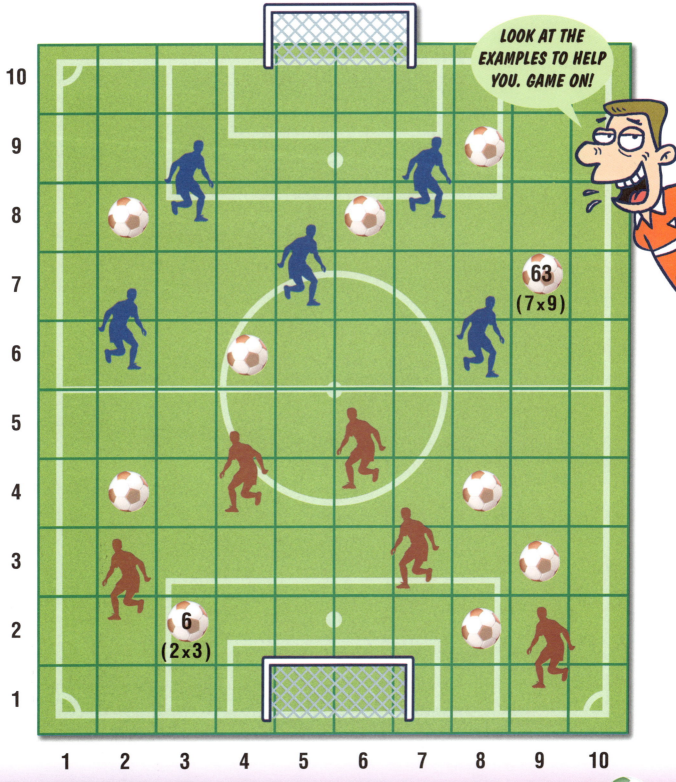

LOOK AT THE EXAMPLES TO HELP YOU. GAME ON!

63 (7 x 9)

6 (2 x 3)

Check your answers and work out your score.

10 times table

The final whistle is about to blow and all you've got left to tackle is the 10 times table. This table is easy - all you need to do is add a 0 to the end of each number. It's in the bag! Count in **10s** and colour in the trophies on the grid. Check out the pattern of numbers when you've finished.

1	2	3	4	5	6	7	8	9	10
11	12	13	14	15	16	17	18	19	20
21	22	23	24	25	26	27	28	29	30
31	32	33	34	35	36	37	38	39	40
41	42	43	44	45	46	47	48	49	50
51	52	53	54	55	56	57	58	59	60
61	62	63	64	65	66	67	68	69	70
71	72	73	74	75	76	77	78	79	80
81	82	83	84	85	86	87	88	89	90
91	92	93	94	95	96	97	98	99	100

1 x 10 = 10

2 x 10 =

3 x 10 =

4 x 10 =

5 x 10 =

6 x 10 =

7 x 10 =

8 x 10 =

9 x 10 =

10 x 10 =

Action Replay

Here's your chance to score 10 winning goals. See if you can complete the table in record time.

ADD THE POINTS TO THE REFEREE'S SCORE CARDS IF YOU NEED HELP. TRY LEARNING THE TABLE OFF BY HEART.

Did you play a blinder?

Top transfer

Fergus Alexsson, manager of Pretend Madrid, has offered these players more money to transfer and play for his team. Alexsson has offered them 10 times as much money per minute of play! Work out their new rate of pay per minute and write it on their new team tops.

£5 x 10 =

£3 x 10 =

£8 x 10 =

£10 x 10 =

Crowd chants

Work out what the crowd is chanting as the final whistle is about to blow!

There goes the final whistle.

F	O	T	P	H	E	I	M	S	A	B	L	G	U
18	48	8	70	60	25	9	28	20	49	32	10	24	100

1. **2 x 4**
2. **6 x 8**
3. **7 x 10**
4. **8 x 6**
5. **9 x 2**

6. **1 x 8**
7. **10 x 6**
8. **5 x 5**
9. **4 x 2**
10. **3 x 3**

11. **4 x 7**
12. **5 x 5**
13. **2 x 10**
14. **8 x 1**
15. **7 x 7**

16. **8 x 4**
17. **5 x 2**
18. **5 x 5**
19. **4 x 5**
20. **1 x 10**

21. **5 x 5**
22. **7 x 7**
23. **3 x 8**
24. **10 x 10**
25. **5 x 5**

1. 2. 3. 4. 5. 6. 7. 8. 9. 10. 11. 12. 13.

14. 15. 16. 17. 18. 19. 20. 21. 22. 23. 24. 25. !

What was your score?

INJURY TIME

Were you a top scorer or do you need to put in some practice? You could be lucky – there's 15 minutes of injury time to play, so get a stopwatch and see if you can solve these multiplications within the time.

1. Multiply 7 by 5.

2. Write four different times table sums that equal 18.

3. In the last 3 games, the referee has shown 5 yellow cards in each game. How many altogether?

4. What is 8 multiplied by 8?

5. If a player has 10 pairs of boots, how many boots does he have altogether?

6. Write four different times table sums that equal 12.

7. If a player eats 7 pieces of orange at every game, how many pieces does he eat over 9 games?

8. $5 \times 4 = \boxed{}$ $5 \times 8 = \boxed{}$ $5 \times 9 = \boxed{}$

9. If a superfan buys 4 programmes at every game and goes to 8 games, how many programmes does she have altogether?

10. Each row in a stadium seats 10 people. How many people would 10 rows seat?

11. If a drink costs £2 and a pie costs £3, how much would 2 pies and 1 drink cost?

12. What is 2 x 2 add 3 x 3?

13. $7 \times 7 = \boxed{}$ $8 \times 8 = \boxed{}$ $9 \times 9 = \boxed{}$

14. Write four different times table sums that equal 20.

15. If a season ticket covers 9 home games, how many home games would 6 season tickets cover?

ANSWERS

Page 2
KICK OFF! 2 times table

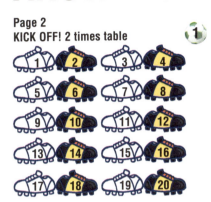

1 x 2 = 2   2 x 2 = 4   3 x 2 = 6
4 x 2 = 8   5 x 2 = 10   6 x 2 = 12
7 x 2 = 14   8 x 2 = 16
9 x 2 = 18   10 x 2 = 20

Page 3

5 x 2 = 10   7 x 2 = 14   3 x 2 = 6

5 x 2 = 10   10 x 2 = 20
7 x 2 = 14   9 x 2 = 18
4 x 2 = 8   6 x 2 = 12

Back of the net

Page 4
3 times table

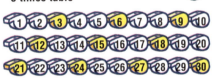

1 x 3 = 3   2 x 3 = 6   3 x 3 = 9
4 x 3 = 12   5 x 3 = 15   6 x 3 = 18
7 x 3 = 21   8 x 3 = 24
9 x 3 = 27   10 x 3 = 30

Page 5
World Cup winners

4 x 3 = 12   5 x 3 = 15   9 x 3 = 27

3 x 3 = 9   6 x 3 = 18   4 x 3 = 12
9 x 3 = 27   7 x 3 = 21   10 x 3 = 30

Corner kick

Page 6
4 times table

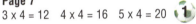

1 x 4 = 4   2 x 4 = 8   3 x 4 = 12
4 x 4 = 16   5 x 4 = 20   6 x 4 = 24
7 x 4 = 28   8 x 4 = 32
9 x 4 = 36   10 x 4 = 40

Page 7

3 x 4 = 12   4 x 4 = 16   5 x 4 = 20

2 x 4 = 8   6 x 4 = 24
4 x 4 = 16   4 x 10 = 40
3 x 4 = 12   4 x 5 = 20

On the ball

Page 8
5 times tables

1	2	3	4	5	6	7	8	9	10
11	12	13	14	15	16	17	18	19	20
21	22	23	24	25	26	27	28	29	30
31	32	33	34	35	36	37	38	39	40
41	42	43	44	45	46	47	48	49	50

1 x 5 = 5   2 x 5 = 10   3 x 5 = 15
4 x 5 = 20   5 x 5 = 25   6 x 5 = 30
7 x 5 = 35   8 x 5 = 40
9 x 5 = 45   10 x 5 = 50

Page 9

5 x 5 = 25   2 x 5 = 10   8 x 5 = 40
Most points - Pretend Madrid.
Least points - Ramshackle Rovers.

EXTRA TIME

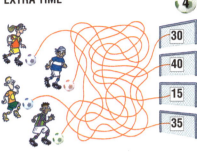

Page 10
6 times tables

1	2	3	4	5	6	7	8	9	10
11	12	13	14	15	16	17	18	19	20
21	22	23	24	25	26	27	28	29	30
31	32	33	34	35	36	37	38	39	40
41	42	43	44	45	46	47	48	49	50
51	52	53	54	55	56	57	58	59	60

1 x 6 = 6   2 x 6 = 12   3 x 6 = 18
4 x 6 = 24   5 x 6 = 30   6 x 6 = 36
7 x 6 = 42   8 x 6 = 48
9 x 6 = 54   10 x 6 = 60

Page 11
Team tactics
OFF-SIDE TRAP

HALF-TIME WHISTLE
Bucket B   Bucket C
4 x 2 = 8 halves   5 x 2 = 10 halves
8 x 6 = 48 pieces   10 x 6 = 60 pieces

Page 12
HALF-TIME ANALYSIS
8 x 2 = 16   6 x 2 = 12   4 x 2 = 8
5 x 3 = 15   2 x 3 = 6   9 x 3 = 27
8 x 4 = 32   7 x 4 = 28   10 x 4 = 40
1 x 5 = 5   9 x 5 = 45   6 x 5 = 30

Trophy takers

Page 13
Get dribbling!

1 x 8 = 8	2 x 8 = 16	3 x 8 = 24
4 x 8 = 32	5 x 8 = 40	6 x 8 = 48
7 x 8 = 56	8 x 8 = 64	
9 x 8 = 72	10 x 8 = 80	

Page 17
Fever pitch!

7 x 8 = 56	9 x 8 = 72	10 x 8 = 80
6 x 8 = 48	2 x 8 = 16	3 x 8 = 24
1 x 8 = 8	5 x 8 = 40	
8 x 8 = 64	4 x 8 = 32	

PENALTY KICK

Page 14
7 times tables

1	2	3	4	5	6	7	8	9	10
11	12	13	14	15	16	17	18	19	20
21	22	23	24	25	26	27	28	29	30
31	32	33	34	35	36	37	38	39	40
41	42	43	44	45	46	47	48	49	50
51	52	53	54	55	56	57	58	59	60
61	62	63	64	65	66	67	68	69	70

1 x 7 = 7	2 x 7 = 14	3 x 7 = 21
4 x 7 = 28	5 x 7 = 35	6 x 7 = 42
7 x 7 = 49	8 x 7 = 56	
9 x 7 = 63	10 x 7 = 70	

Page 15
Sliding tackles

4 x 7 = 28	2 x 7 = 14
7 x 7 = 49	5 x 7 = 35

Keepy-uppy
42 63 49 14 21 35 70 56

Page 16
8 times tables

Page 18
9 times tables

1 x 9 = 9	2 x 9 = 18	3 x 9 = 27
4 x 9 = 36	5 x 9 = 45	6 x 9 = 54
7 x 9 = 63	8 x 9 = 72	
9 x 9 = 81	10 x 9 = 90	

Page 19
Spot the balls

Page 20
10 times tables

1	2	3	4	5	6	7	8	9	10
11	12	13	14	15	16	17	18	19	20
21	22	23	24	25	26	27	28	29	30
31	32	33	34	35	36	37	38	39	40
41	42	43	44	45	46	47	48	49	50
51	52	53	54	55	56	57	58	59	60
61	62	63	64	65	66	67	68	69	70
71	72	73	74	75	76	77	78	79	80
81	82	83	84	85	86	87	88	89	90
91	92	93	94	95	96	97	98	99	100

1 x 10 =10	2 x 10 = 20	3 x 10 = 30
4 x 10 = 40	5 x 10 = 50	6 x 10 = 60
7 x 10 = 70	8 x 10 = 80	
9 x 10 = 90	10 x 10 = 100	

Page 21
Top transfer

£5 x 10 = £50	£3 x 10 = £30
£8 x 10 = £80	£10 x 10 = £100

Crowd chants
TOP OF THE TIMES TABLES LEAGUE!

Page 22
INJURY TIME
1. 35
2. Any four of the following:
18 x 1 1 x 18 6 x 3 3 x 6 2 x 9 9 x 2.
3. 15 altogether
4. 64
5. 20
6. Any four of the following:
12 x 1 1 x 12 4 x 3 3 x 4 6 x 2 2 x 6.
7. 63 pieces
8. 5 x 4 = 20 5 x 8 = 40 5 x 9 = 45
9. 32 programmes
10. 100 people
11. £8
12. 4 + 9 = 13
13. 7 x 7 = 49 8 x 8 = 64 9 x 9 = 81
14. Any four of the following:
20 x 1 1 x 20 5 x 4 4 x 5 2 x 10
10 x 2.
15. 54 games